The Da Vinci Quiz

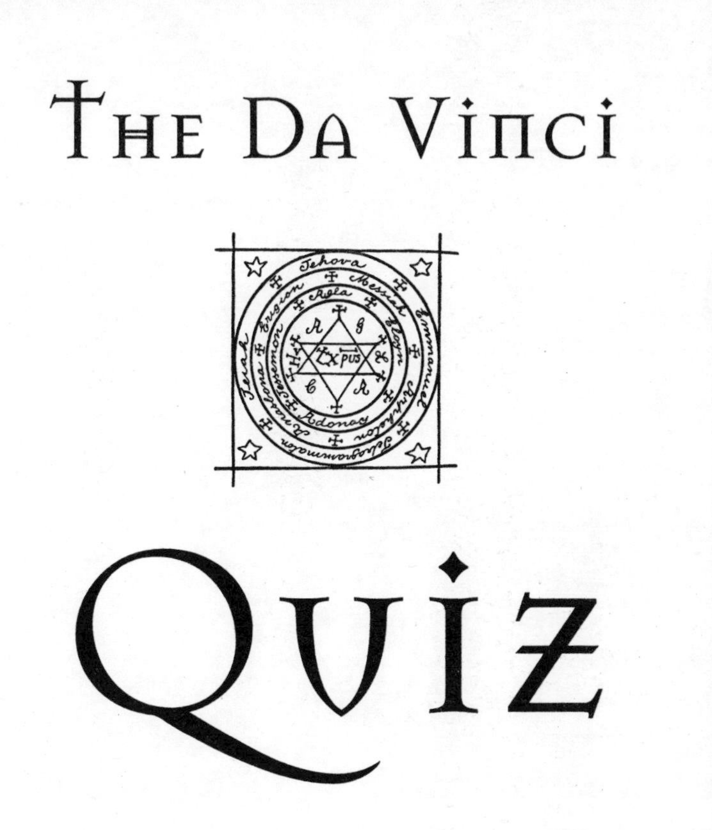

A writer, editor, and quiz-book compiler, **Tracey Turner** has always been fascinated by mysteries, codes, and puzzles. As a result, she quickly became drawn in to the intriguing world of Dan Brown's *The Da Vinci Code*, and began to ask herself questions about the facts behind the fiction—the results of her search for answers form the basis for the 501 questions in this book. She has published ten books for adults and children, and lives in Londo

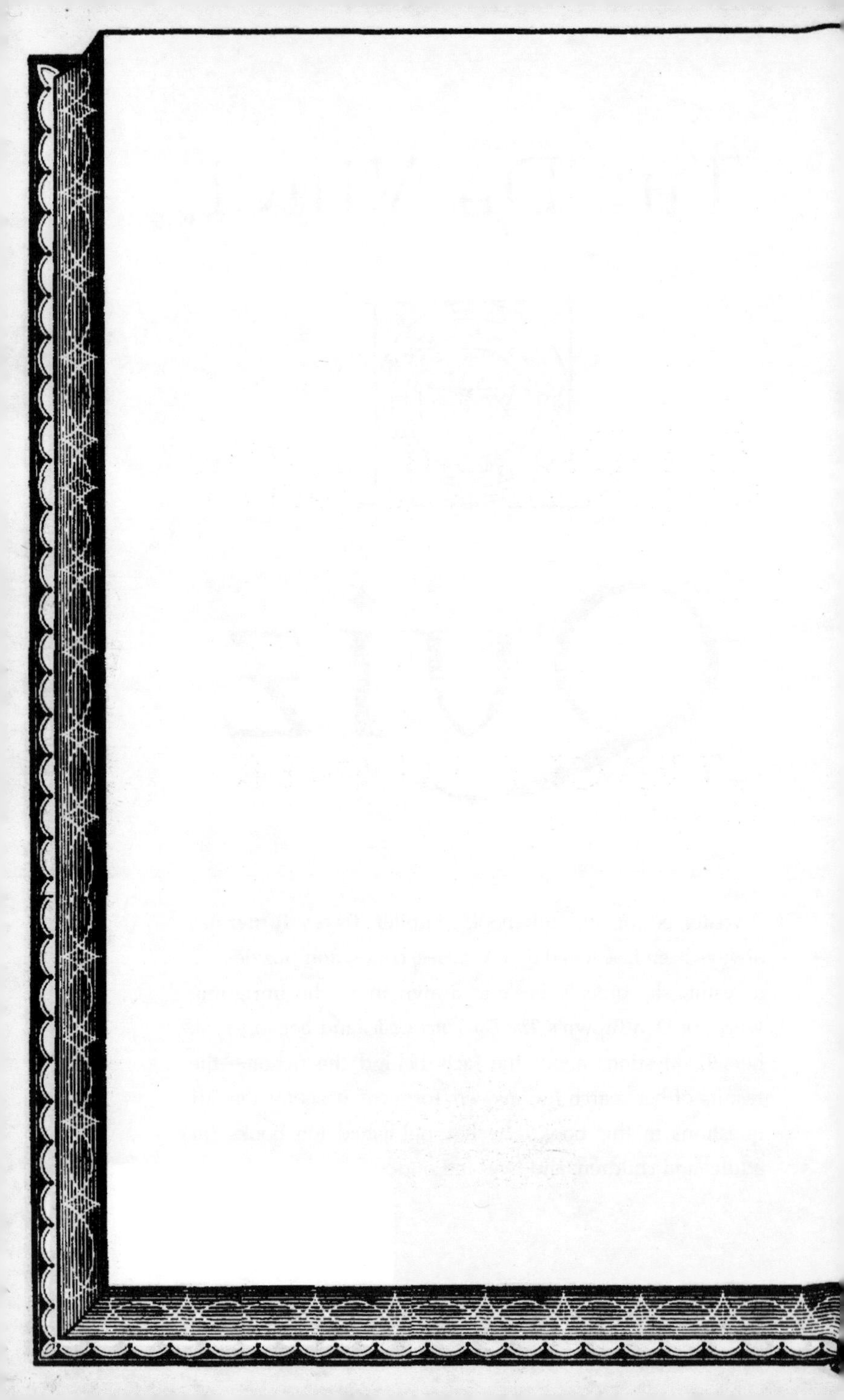

The Da Vinci Quiz

501 Questions to Crack the Code

TRACEY TURNER

First Edition for North America published in 2005 by
Barron's Educational Series, Inc.

Conceived, designed, and produced by
Michael O'Mara Books Limited
9 Lion Yard, Tremadoc Road
London SW4 7NQ

All inquiries should be addressed to:
Barron's Educational Series, Inc.
250 Wireless Boulevard
Hauppauge, New York 11788
www.barronseduc.com

International Standard Book No. 13: 978-0-7641-3328-2
International Standard Book No. 10: 0-7641-3328-4

Library of Congress Catalog Card No. 2005926322

Designed and typeset by Design 23
Cover design by www.glensaville.com

Printed and bound in Great Britain
9 8 7 6 5 4 3 2 1

Introduction

The Da Vinci Code, by Dan Brown, is a phenomenal success, primarily because of its controversial and fascinating subject matter. The book's plot is a modern-day search for the Holy Grail, which turns out to be a prize far stranger than the sacred chalice of legend.

Although the novel is a work of fiction it claims a basis in fact, and it is this "real world" of *The Da Vinci Code* that has intrigued millions of fans across the globe. Readers have become fascinated with secret societies, the papacy, religious orders, and works of art that might provide coded messages pointing to a great Christian conspiracy. The increase in tourism to places such as the Louvre Museum and Saint–Sulpice Church in Paris, Westminster Abbey in London, and Rosslyn Chapel in Scotland is testimony to the extraordinary interest in the real places visited in the novel.

The 501 questions in this book follow the physical journey taken by the fictional characters in *The Da Vinci Code,* stopping off in Paris, London,

Scotland, and Rome, with brief detours to Jerusalem, Florence, and New York City. It also follows their journey through the mysterious world of ancient scrolls, codes and ciphers, crusading knights, pagan worship, and the Sacred Feminine. These questions will test your understanding of *The Da Vinci Code* and the real world that it claims to inhabit, but be warned: Not all the answers are in the novel, although many will be found in general knowledge or through knowledge of the many disparate elements that contribute to Dan Brown's thriller.

TRACEY TURNER
London, May 2005

The Questions

1. Which airfield lies nineteen miles southeast of central London?

2. What are Robert Boyle, Victor Hugo, and Claude Debussy supposed to have had in common?

3. Which of Leonardo da Vinci's artworks was fired at by Napoleon's troops when they occupied Milan?

4. True or false: The Western Schism that split the Christian Church in the fourteenth century resulted in the election of three rival popes.

5. In the New Testament, who is the first person to meet the resurrected Christ?

6. Which religious–military organization was dissolved by a papal bull issued by Pope Clement V in 1307?

7. Which religious body has its British residence at 5 Orme Court, Bayswater, London?

8. What was unusual about the reign of Pope John Paul I?

9. Which Renaissance man designed flying machines, among them a helicopter?

10. Which twentieth-century Spanish surrealist artist painted *The Persistence of Memory*?

11. Which of Christ's apostles was originally called Simon?

12. From what does London University's King's College get its name?

13. Which Italian city has an airport named after Leonardo da Vinci?

14. Which early Christian texts were found in an Egyptian cave in 1945?

15. Who wrote, "Many have made a trade of delusions and false miracles, deceiving the stupid multitude"?

16. Which controversial Parisian structure was built in 1989?

17. Which Islamic place of worship is built on the Temple Mount in Jerusalem?

18. In the Bible, an earthquake breaks open the prison where Paul the Apostle and his companion are held. What is the name of Paul's companion?

19. What links the Knights Templar to "unlucky" Friday the thirteenth?

20. Who "explored the course and figures of the planets, the paths of comets, the tides of the sea," according to an inscription on a memorial in Westminster Abbey?

21. True or false: Leonardo da Vinci designed a submarine.

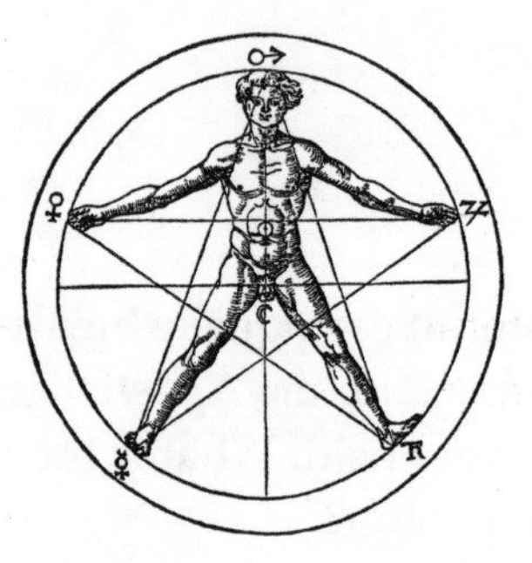

22. What is ODAN?

23. In which book of the Old Testament are the words "Hitherto shalt thou come, but no further"?

24. What is the meaning of the Latin phrase *castigo corpus meum*?

25. Which papal residence was originally built as a palace by the emperor Domitian?

26. In which Scottish church can you find depictions of the pagan Green Man?

27. Which high-tech Parisian building, completed in 1977, is made of steel and glass and houses modern art?

28. Which Parisian church has recently posted a notice declaring that it is not "a vestige of a pagan temple"?

29. Which famous artist described the human body as "the ultimate machine"?

30. What is the name of the huge Ferris wheel–like structure on London's South Bank?

31. Which seventeenth-century artist painted *The Temptation of Saint Anthony* and is the subject of a book by Saunière in *The Da Vinci Code*?

32. Which Italian castle is perched 450 yards above Lago d'Albano?

33. Which Christian church stands on what is thought to be the site of Jesus's tomb?

34. What does the Latin phrase *opus dei* mean?

35. Which famous artwork is known in Italian as *Cenacolo Vinciano*?

36. Which of Jesus's apostles denied him three times before the cock crowed twice?

37. Exeter Cathedral in southwestern England claimed to have one of the fingers (until it was lost during the Reformation) of which female saint?

38. Which of the following statements is false: Godefroi de Bouillon was a French king. The Priory of Sion's Grand Master resigned in 1984. A Muslim place of worship stands on Temple Mount.

39. What is the technical phrase used in the church to describe a feast like Easter, that does not occur on the same day each year?

40. In which group of "lost" Gospels do we learn that Jesus frequently kissed Mary Magdalene?

41. By what name is the Vatican's Institute for Religious Works commonly known?

42. True or false: Godefroi de Bouillon founded the Knights Templar.

43. Which of Christ's apostles betrayed him for thirty pieces of silver?

44. Which French president was partly responsible for the construction of the Louvre pyramid?

45. Who painted *Genevra da Benci* as well as an Annunciation?

46. What connects Dolly the sheep, the world's first cloned animal, with Rosslyn Chapel?

47. True or false: Opus Dei had several members in the government of the Spanish dictator General Franco.

48. Whose letters make up fourteen books of the New Testament?

49. *Vicarius Christi* is one of whose formal titles?

50. Which English scientist and mathematician pushed a pointed stick into his eye socket as one of his experiments with light?

51. The Knights Templar was one of two religious orders of military knights during the Crusades. What was the other one?

52. Where is the tomb of Saint Peter?

53. Which is the older organization, the Knights Templar or the Priory of Sion?

54. In 1956, someone threw a rock at and damaged which famous painting in the Louvre?

55. What does the French phrase *ne pas déranger* mean?

56. What is the title of the best-selling book by Michael Baigent, Richard Leigh, and Henry Lincoln from which *The Da Vinci Code* draws many of its background elements?

57. The Golden Ratio, or Divine Proportion, is known by which Greek letter?

58. Josemaría Escrivá founded which religious organization in 1928?

59. Which of Leonardo's masterpieces was completed in 1497 in Milan, where it may still be seen?

60. What is the trademarked name of a tough, transparent, protective material often used in place of glass?

61. What is the *Codex Leicester*?

62. *Philosophiae Naturalis Principia Mathematica,* often simply called the *Principia,* is the work of which famous scientist?

63. According to legend, who caught Christ's blood in the Holy Grail and later brought the cup to Glastonbury in the west of England?

64. Who was Lisa Gherardini?

65. Pope Alexander VI was a member of which infamous medieval Italian family?

66. Which ancient city did Constantine the Great name Nova Roma but came to be called Constantinople after him?

67. Which painting did Leonardo take with him when he traveled?

68. Which of the four New Testament Gospels refers to its narrator as "the one whom Jesus loved"?

69. What is the derivation of the name Magdalene?

70. Which Paris institution has a historic building on the Rue de Richelieu and a modern complex at Quai François-Mauriac?

71. In which Italian city is the Uffizi Gallery?

72. Why did Biggin Hill airfield in Kent become famous in the Battle of Britain during the Second World War?

73. Who is the current British Royal Historian?

74. What is the practical purpose of the Louvre's Pyramide Inversée?

75. True or false: Isaac Newton, experimenting with alchemy, attempted to turn base metals into gold.

76. What is a cilice?

77. Where can you find representations of the Empress, the Hermit, and the Star?

78. True or false: The Uffizi Gallery removed *The Adoration of the Magi* from its walls after the art expert Maurizio Seracini's discoveries, because it did not want to reveal the painting's true meaning.

79. Who ostensibly resigned as the Grand Master of the Priory of Sion in 1984?

80. What is the name of the ancient cipher that uses a substitution system of Hebrew letters?

81. The early Christian church wrongly depicted Mary Magdalene as what?

82. In which Parisian church was the Marquis de Sade baptized and Victor Hugo married?

83. Who painted *The Garden of Earthly Delights*?

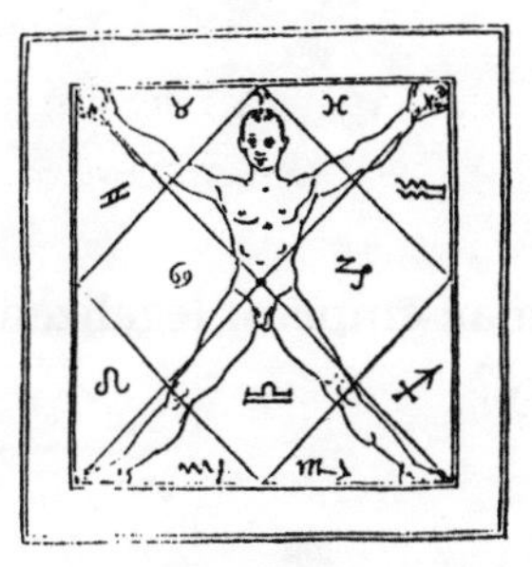

84. Where can one find 135 brass medallions marked Arago set into the ground?

85. Whose monument includes representations of the signs of the zodiac, a telescope, and a prism?

86. True or false: The Knights Templar built Rosslyn Chapel.

87. What does DCPJ stand for?

88. Which Roman emperor legalized Christianity?

89. Which French president had the nickname the Sphinx?

90. Who were also known as the Poor Knights of Christ?

91. Which Parisian church is famous for its organ, the largest in Europe?

92. The word *gargoyle* comes from the Old French word *gargouille*, meaning what?

93. What is odd about the *Mona Lisa*'s eyebrows?

94. Who is known as the first Christian emperor?

95. Which noted English scientist of the seventeenth and eighteenth centuries also devoted much time to the study of alchemy?

96. What are the names of Rome's two international airports?

97. Which one of Leonardo's most famous subjects was also painted by the Venetian painter Jacopo Bassano?

98. Although it is painted on a wall, why is it incorrect to describe *The Last Supper* as a fresco?

99. True or false: The Place du Carrousel in Paris was once the site of nature-worship rituals.

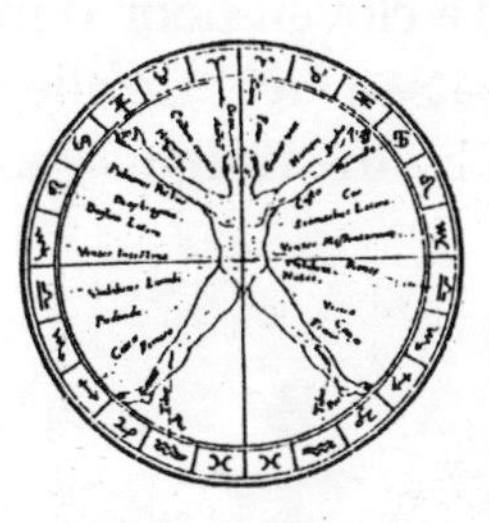

100. True or false: The Depository Bank of Zurich in Paris is a real-life financial institution.

101. Who painted *The Birth of Venus* and is listed as a Grand Master of the Priory of Sion in the *Dossiers Secrets*?

102. What would have prevented Walt Disney himself from putting messages about the Sacred Feminine into the films *The Little Mermaid* and *The Lion King*?

103. In modern occult lore, which pagan deity is described as a cloven-hoofed man with the head of a goat—a creature allegedly worshipped by the Knights Templar?

104. What is a *crux gemmata*?

105. Which legendary English king is associated with the Holy Grail and Glastonbury?

106. According to legend, in which ancient city (in present-day Turkey) did the Virgin Mary live after the Crucifixion?

107. Which British church is also known as the Cathedral of Codes?

108. Which ancient Egyptian god was born on December 25?

109. What is the name of Paris's most famous higher-education institution?

110. True or false: In the New Testament, Jesus never refers to himself as "the son of God".

111. Which famous painting languished for twenty-seven months at the bottom of a trunk?

112. What is the name of the ancient Roman goddess of love?

113. Which famous scrolls containing important religious texts were found near Jerusalem in 1947?

114. Where can one find a silver disk marking the site of Jesus's cross?

115. Pope Clement V, who helped to suppress the Templars, moved the seat of the papacy from Rome to a city in his native France. Which city?

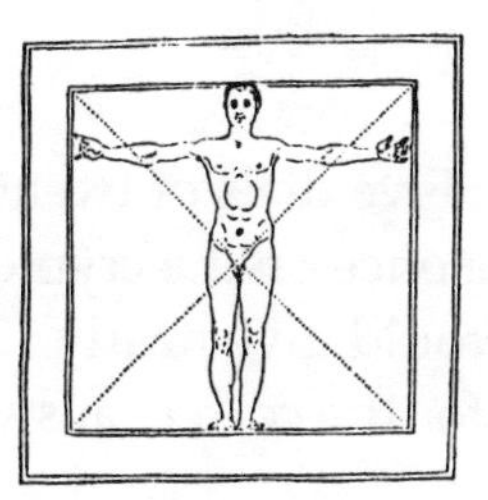

116. True or false: The ancient Egyptian goddess Isis was also known as L'Isa.

117. What is the world's smallest independent state?

118. From what did the Knights Templar take their name?

119. Which major river flows from east to west through Paris?

120. True or false: Five dials of twenty-six letters each (like the ones on the cryptex in *The Da Vinci Code*) would give nearly 12 million possibilities for the correct answer?

121. Which famous artist injected human hearts with wax and made anatomical sketches of them?

122. Which London church is modeled on the Church of the Holy Sepulchre in Jerusalem?

123. Who is the astronomer commemorated in the 135 brass plaques marking the original prime meridian line in Paris?

124. Which Merovingian king was assassinated on the orders of Pépin the Fat?

125. Which organization's U.S. headquarters has separate entrances on separate streets for men and women?

126. True or false: Pope Urban VI tortured and executed his cardinals and was known as "the Mad Pope".

127. Which Parisian park was commissioned by Catherine de' Medici in the sixteenth century?

128. Which Shakespeare tragedy is the first play in his Roman series?

129. True or false: The Dead Sea Scrolls are some of the earliest Christian scriptures.

130. Which British queen was caught sending enciphered messages plotting to overthrow Queen Elizabeth I?

131. Who converted to Christianity after seeing a vision on the road to Damascus?

132. Where is Poets' Corner?

133. Who wears the Fisherman's Ring?

134. Which knights were among the chief moneylenders in the East during the Crusades?

135. The supposed murder of which real-life pope formed part of the plot of the movie *Godfather III*?

136. What is the name of the historic airfield outside Paris where the Paris Air Show takes place every two years?

137. What is the name of the pope's summer residence?

138. Which zodiac sign is represented by a bull?

139. Which London University college is situated west of the capital in Egham, Surrey?

140. In which room in the Louvre does the *Mona Lisa* hang?

141. What is the Greek term for the irrational number 1.618033989?

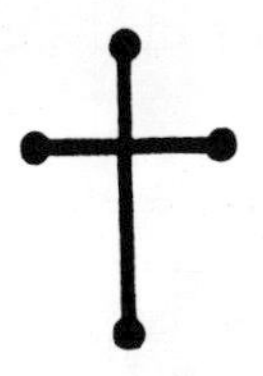

142. True or false: The Louvre pyramid contains 666 panes of glass.

143. Which London park, a place of rendezvous in *The Da Vinci Code,* was a leper colony during the Middle Ages?

144. Who derived the inverse-square law?

145. At which tourist attraction on the south bank of the Thames River can one climb into a capsule for a bird's-eye view of London?

146. Whom do many Christians honor as the first pope?

147. What is special about the French Merovingian dynasty, according to *The Da Vinci Code*?

148. True or false: The Gospel of Mary Magdalene is one of the Gnostic Gospels.

149. In which church in Paris is there a stained-glass window with the initials *P* and *S* in the center?

150. Which painting's Italian name is *La Gioconda*?

151. The Knights Templar were associated with the Johnite heresy, which preached the worship of whom above Jesus Christ?

152. True or false: In terms of fuel economy, a SmartCar gets 100 miles to the gallon.

153. What are the four suits in a tarot deck?

154. What is the meaning of the Greek word from which *pentagram* is derived?

155. Which military commander contributed looted works of art to the Louvre, some of which were returned to their original owners after the Battle of Waterloo?

156. What did the art diagnostician Maurizio Seracini discover when he examined Leonardo's *The Adoration of the Magi*?

157. Who composed *The Magic Flute*?

158. Pilgrims visit a church in Saint-Maximin-la-Ste-Baume, in southeastern France, to kneel before the bones of which follower of Christ?

159. Which London hospital is the nearest to Orme Court in Bayswater?

160. Where can you find the elaborate Apprentice (or Prentice) Pillar?

161. What was the Council of Nicaea?

162. How many people are depicted in Leonardo's *Last Supper*?

163. What is the English name for the Italian city of Firenze?

164. Which London church was built by the Knights Templar?

165. Which book, written in the fifteenth century as a sort of handbook for witch hunters, states, among other things, that gossip is enough evidence to bring a suspected witch to trial and recommends the use of torture?

166. What is Mount Moriah in Jerusalem also known as?

167. Which god, worshipped throughout the Roman Empire at the time of Christ, was born on December 25?

168. In which part of the Louvre are fashion shows sometimes held?

169. Which seventeenth-century French artist painted *The Shepherds of Arcadia* and *The Adoration of the Golden Calf* and in *The Da Vinci Code* is Saunière's second-favorite painter?

170. True or false: The Vatican Secret Archives are closed to everyone except the pope, cardinals, and bishops.

171. Who was Jacques de Molay?

172. Which key Christian event is found in the Gospels of Matthew, Luke, and John but is missing from the Gospel of Mark?

173. Which of Leonardo da Vinci's masterpieces has deteriorated and been restored so much that it now contains almost none of the artist's original paint?

174. Which foreign educational establishment has its campus in six buildings in the seventh arrondissement of Paris?

175. True or false: The ancient Greek Olympic Games were held in honor of the goddess Venus.

176. Where in London might one find stone effigies of Templar knights?

177. Which ancient Greek god carries a trident, sometimes said to be the origin of the devil's pitchfork?

178. "Vile meaningless doodles" is an anagram of *Les Demoiselles d'Avignon*, a painting by which artist?

179. Which of the following statements is false: Saint-Sulpice was originally a temple to the ancient Egyptian goddess Isis. Brass medallions mark the original prime meridian in Paris's streets. The Louvre was originally built as a fortress.

180. True or false: The Diana, Princess of Wales Memorial Walk in Kensington Gardens is lined with the symbol of a rose.

181. What city did Constantine the Great dedicate to Christ?

182. In which language are the Gnostic Gospels written?

183. The Jardin des Tuileries in Paris gets its name from which commodity that used to be manufactured there?

184. Why is it impossible for Rosslyn Chapel to be a replica of Solomon's Temple?

185. True or false: The *Dossiers Secrets*, the alleged "documents" of the Priory of Sion, were deposited in the Bibliothèque Nationale in Paris in the nineteenth century.

186. What does the piece of jewelry known as a *crux gemmata* represent?

187. Which place of worship lies between Fleet Street and the Thames River in London?

188. Which seventeenth-century artist painted *The Penitent Magdalene*?

189. Why did Vincenzo Peruggia steal the *Mona Lisa* from the Louvre in 1911?

190. True or false: Thirty-nine of Leonardo da Vinci's paintings are still in existence.

191. What famous Roman saw a vision of a flaming cross along with the words "By this, Conquer"?

192. Which of the four evangelists has more than one book in the New Testament?

193. True or false: The Vatican's Italian embassy is actually located in Italy.

194. Who, according to the best evidence, founded the Priory of Sion in the 1950s?

195. Where would you find the Major Arcana and the Minor Arcana?

196. What is the Bois de Boulogne?

197. The Gospel of Sophia of Jesus Christ, reproductions of which are found in Sir Leigh Teabing's study, is one of which group of Gospels?

198. Who was the first non-Italian to be elected pope in nearly five hundred years?

199. *Clef de voûte* is a French term for which architectural feature?

200. Like the fictional Sir Leigh Teabing, Rudy Giuliani, the former mayor of New York City, is a member of a British order of knighthood. Why is Giuliani not addressed as "Sir Rudy"?

201. How many stone effigies of knights are there in Temple Church?

202. What is a Beechcraft Baron 58?

203. True or false: The fleur-de-lis was used as a symbol by the Priory of Sion.

204. In which square in Paris is a seventy-five-foot-tall ancient Egyptian obelisk located?

205. Amon was one of the most important gods of which ancient civilization?

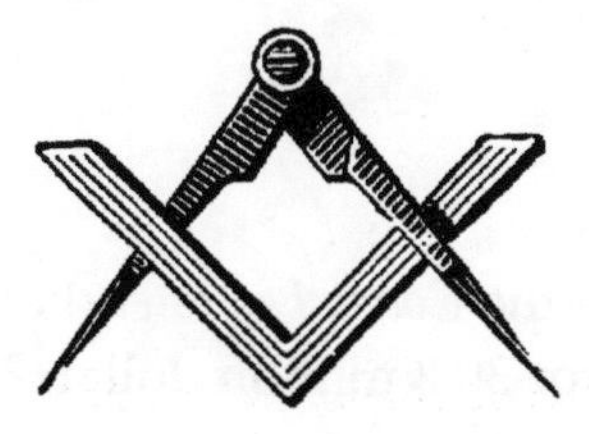

206. What is unusual about the national flag of Switzerland, which displays an equal-armed cross?

207. Which architect designed the Louvre pyramid?

208. After it was damaged in the Great Fire of London in 1666, Temple Church was restored by which famous architect?

209. True or false: The Priory of Sion was registered as a social club with the French government.

210. Who owns the *Codex Leicester*, having bought it for 30.8 million dollars?

211. Following a decision to celebrate Easter every year on the date that had been decided at the Council of Nicaea, the Julian calendar was recalculated, and a new calendar system was implemented in 1582. What was the name of this new calendar?

212. What American institution of higher education was founded in France in 1962?

213. Why is it incorrect to refer to Leonardo da Vinci, the great Italian painter, sculptor, architect, and engineer, as da Vinci?

214. In the book *Holy Blood, Holy Grail,* it is suggested that the story in the New Testament of the Wedding at Cana, at which water was turned into wine, is an account of whose alleged marriage?

215. Where are Geoffrey Chaucer, Charles Dickens, and Thomas Hardy buried?

216. What are the *Dossiers Secrets*?

217. Who designed a parachute in the early sixteenth century?

218. In which language was the Atbash Cipher written?

219. Which English queen is buried in a tomb with her halfsister, Mary I, under a canopied marble monument in Westminster Abbey's Lady Chapel?

220. Which modern-day movement, seen by its followers as a religion and sometimes associated with "white witches," is based on pre-Christian traditions and includes worship of a deity known as the Goddess?

221. Where are the Holy Grail, gospels written by Christ, the Ark of the Covenant, the Knights Templars' treasure, and Jesus's embalmed head all supposed to be buried?

222. One of Leonardo's versions of *Madonna of the Rocks* hangs in the Louvre. Where is the other version of the painting?

223. True or false: Mary Magdalene is mentioned fifty-four times in the New Testament.

224. Which group raised questions about the nature of Jesus's divinity and was excommunicated on charges of heresy after the Council of Nicaea?

225. Which part of the following statement is false: Leonardo da Vinci designed a giant crossbow; a cryptex, a device for keeping messages from being intercepted; and a tank (i.e., an armored vehicle).

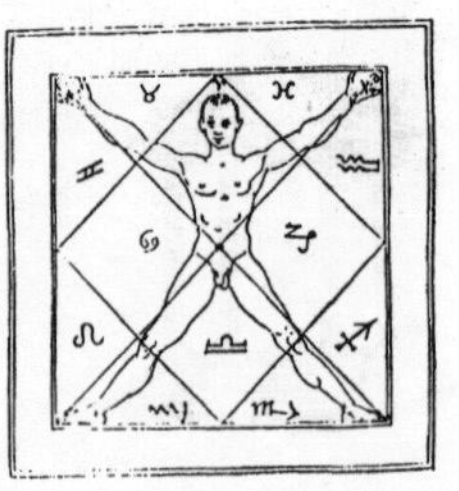

226. What is the meaning of the Spanish expression, '*Hago la obra de Dios*'?

227. Who was Abu Yusuf Ismail al-Kindi?

228. Why is Isaac Newton associated with an apple?

229. Which Parisian art museum is housed in an old train station?

230. What is the name of Dan Brown's previous novel featuring Robert Langdon?

231. Which independent state was created in 1929?

232. Which organization has its U.S. headquarters at 243 Lexington Avenue, New York City?

233. True or false: The antipope Clement VII was also known as "the Butcher of Cesena".

234. From which Parisian station would you catch a train to Lille?

235. Which London park is overlooked not only by Opus Dei's London residence but also by Kensington Palace, home of the late Diana, Princess of Wales?

236. Which religious organization was founded on October 2, 1928?

237. True or false: Inside Rosslyn Chapel, there is a star-shaped pathway worn into the floor by centuries of footsteps.

238. Which 1999 film portrays a secret society engaging in *hieros gamos*?

239. Which city was the capital of Italy until 1869?

240. Which soldiers are responsible for the safety of the pope within the Vatican?

241. The Tomb of the Unknown Soldier lies underneath which Parisian monument?

242. In the early sixteenth century, which famous artist designed and made a suit of armor that could stand up and sit down by itself?

243. Which French writer, artist, and filmmaker is listed in the *Dossiers Secrets* as a Priory of Sion Grand Master?

244. Inspired by the stunning architecture of the former station, Gare Saint–Lazare is the subject of a painting by which Impressionist artist?

245. Which companion of Paul the Apostle is described as one of the "leading men among the brethren"?

246. When did the Catholic Church retract its statement that Mary Magdalene was a prostitute?

247. True or false: Despite being called the Poor Knights of Christ (and their emblem being two knights riding one horse), the Knights Templar became rich in both money and land.

248. The fictional Bishop Aringarosa has an unusual surname. What is an approximate translation of the Italian words *aringa rosa*?

249. Which cathedral in northern France contains a Black Madonna, zodiacal and other pagan imagery, and a famous labyrinth?

250. What is the name of the twelfth-century Italian mathematician who created the series of numbers in which each number is the sum of the two preceding ones?

251. Which institution, described in *The Da Vinci Code* as the most secure library on earth, was made separate from the Vatican Library in the seventeenth century?

252. Where is the *Venus de Milo* exhibited?

253. The painting called the *Last Judgement* is housed within London's Westminster Abbey, but in which specific building?

254. What is the name of the general council in the 1960s at which Catholic leaders attempted to modernize the attitudes of the Roman Catholic Church?

255. In the Gospel of Matthew, about whom is Jesus talking when he says, "On this rock I will build my church"?

256. True or false: Those suffering from albinism are legally blind.

257. True or false: Alexander Pope gave a eulogy at the funeral of Sir Isaac Newton.

258. What is the Collegiate Church of Saint Peter in London also known as?

259. Which Parisian landmark was built in 1889 to celebrate the centenary of the French Revolution?

260. In which Gospel is Jesus asked why he loves Mary Magdalene more than the other disciples?

261. In which supposed Templar construction can you find carvings of saints, biblical characters, kings and queens, dragons, unicorns, and monkeys?

262. In which ancient city in modern-day Turkey might you visit what is supposed to be the Virgin Mary's house?

263. Which of Bill Gates's possessions is on display in the Seattle Art Museum and has been made into a CD?

264. Which of the following statements is false: *The Adoration of the Magi* was never finished. The *Mona Lisa* was stolen in 1911. *The Last Supper* was denounced as a heresy when it was finished.

265. What is the name of Josemaría Escrivá's book, central to the beliefs of Opus Dei members?

266. Which Egyptian goddess is sometimes pictured with her infant son Horus?

267. During the fourteenth century the pope's residence was not in Rome. Where was it?

268. In the eleventh century Westminster Abbey was known as the "west minster" to distinguish it from the east minster. What was the "east minster"?

269. What is the Arago Line that Robert Langdon follows through Paris?

270. Which of the New Testament Gospels is thought to have been the first to be written?

271. What is represented by the Greek letter phi?

272. True or false: From the window of the restroom at the western end of the Grand Gallery in the Louvre can be seen the Eiffel Tower, the Arc de Triomphe, and the dome of Sacré-Coeur.

273. Where are the world headquarters of Opus Dei?

274. In which film did Willem Dafoe play Christ and Barbara Hershey play Mary Magdalene?

275. Where is the Denon Wing?

276. Which French king was responsible for persecuting the Knights Templar in 1307?

277. True or false: The word *cilice* originally meant "hair shirt".

278. Who is Eros?

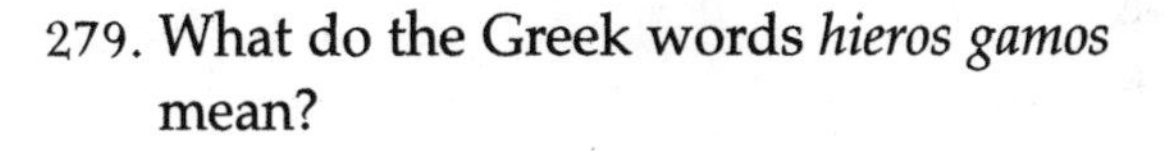

279. What do the Greek words *hieros gamos* mean?

280. Which independent state has its own currency, flag, postage stamps, and bank yet fewer than a thousand citizens?

281. What is the name of the creed, still recited in many Christian liturgies, that was drafted and adopted in 325 C.E. at a meeting of bishops presided over by the emperor Constantine?

282. True or false: The university subject and discipline Symbology was concocted by Dan Brown and does not exist.

283. Which dynasty of French kings first invaded Paris in the sixth century?

284. The earliest written work about the Holy Grail dates from which century?

285. Who was the child born to Ser Piero and Caterina?

286. True or false: The Vatican Bank enjoys immunity from Italian law and banking regulations.

287. What did the pentagram represent when it was used as a Christian symbol?

288. What became the official residence of the pope at the end of the fourteenth century?

289. True or false: Five million women were burned at the stake during three hundred years of witch hunts.

290. In a religious context, what is the purpose of self-mortification?

291. What is the city of Constantinople called today?

292. What is the name for the central stone in an arch?

293. True or false: College Garden, in the grounds of Westminster Abbey, was once used by its monastic community as an area to practice archery?

294. Which Gospel begins, "In the beginning was the Word, and the Word was with God, and the Word was God"?

295. According to *The Da Vinci Code,* Godefroi de Bouillon is supposed to have founded which organization in 1099?

296. By what name do some scholars call the hypothetical missing documents of Christ's teachings—possibly written in his own hand?

297. What are the oldest known Christian documents?

298. In which famous London park can Duck Island be found: Hyde Park, Kensington Gardens or Saint James's Park?

299. (*Left*) When visiting this historic London church, you may encounter a lawyer. Why?

300. (*Below*) An early artist's impression of biblical Jerusalem. How is the building in the center connected to the Knights Templar?

301. (*Above*) Leonardo painted *The Last Supper* using a type of pigment that could be mixed with water, usually in the form of egg yolk. What is the name for this mixture?

302. (*Left*) This wooded park on the western edge of Paris has a somewhat unsavory character at night. What is its name?

303. (*Left*) Photographed in Paris, this car is built by which famous European manufacturer?

304. (*Left*) This octagonal hall is part of Westminster Abbey in London and, before the Houses of Parliament were built, it was the site where the English Parliament met. What is its name?

305. (*Right*) The pillars shown in this nineteenth-century engraving are in which British church?

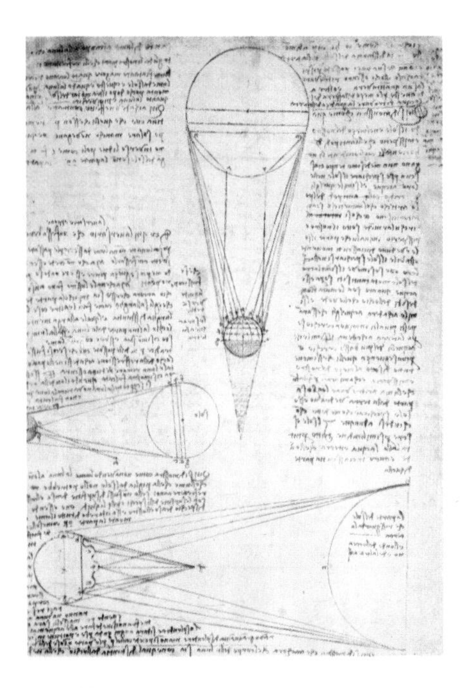

306. (*Left*) This page of notes by Leonardo da Vinci is from a manuscript bought by an English nobleman in 1717. What is the name given to the manuscript?

307. (*Below left*) This massive Parisian monument was built to honor the Emperor Napoleon's military successes. What is its name?

308. (*Below*) What is the name of this pagan deity, said to have been idolatrously worshipped by the Knights Templar?

309. (*Above*) This document is one of a large number of ancient religious texts discovered in a period from 1947 to the mid-1950s, and dating from around the time of Christ. The authors were members of an ascetic Jewish sect; what was its name?

310. (*Right*) A detail from Leonardo's most famous work, the *Mona Lisa*. What material is the enigmatic portrait painted on?

311. (*Above left*) This engraving shows part of a memorial to a great British genius. Where can it be found?

312. (*Above*) The white marble obelisk on the left forms part of a device designed to record certain astronomical data. Where can it be seen?

313. (*Left*) Why would this man have called himself "poor", regardless of his own wealth?

314. (*Right*) In which deck, used for fortune-telling and for certain games, would you find these playing cards?

315. (*Below*) This painting by the seventeenth-century French artist Nicolas Poussin shows the court of which biblical king connected to the Knights Templar?

316. (*Above*) The Pyramid at the entrance to the Louvre Museum in Paris. How many triangular pools surround it?

317. (*Below*) Which of these two versions of Leonardo's *Madonna of the Rocks* is the earlier painting, A or B?

A

B

318. Which Leonardo da Vinci masterpiece was protected during the Second World War by sandbags, which minimized the damage from a bomb blast in 1943?

319. The medieval alchemist Nicholas Flamel is supposed to have been the head of which organization?

320. Who is recognized as the first Christian martyr and has a "pugilistic" international holiday named after him?

321. Which bridge crosses the Thames River in London between Waterloo and Southwark Bridges and is used as a landmark by Teabing as he travels to Temple Church?

322. Which twentieth-century American artist is most famous for her paintings of blossoming flowers, among them *Oriental Poppies*, *Light Iris*, and *Jack-in-the-Pulpit*?

323. Which city-state has two official languages: Latin and Swiss German?

324. The harsh penalties prescribed by the Athenian legislator Draco in the seventh century B.C.E., often for trivial crimes, gave rise to which word meaning "severe" or "exceedingly strict"?

325. The Louvre displays approximately 24,000 pieces of art, but how many does it actually own?

326. True or false: The swastika represents a cross revolving like a wheel, and before it was appropriated by the Nazis, it was a symbol for good.

327. In which state do men account for nearly 100 percent of the permanent residents?

328. Whose tomb lies in the Chapel of Saint-Hubert in Amboise, France?

329. How many books are there in the New Testament?

330. Which seventeenth-century château, located just outside Paris and featured in *The Da Vinci Code*, now offers tours through its rooms?

331. What language did Jesus speak?

332. In which century was the Priory of Sion founded?

333. Which octagonal chamber held meetings of the English Parliament in the fourteenth and fifteenth centuries?

334. Who was elected and to what office on April 19, 2005 at the age of seventy-eight?

335. What or who is Baphomet, whose alleged worship by the Knights Templar led to the order's downfall?

336. Which of the following statements is false: The knightly Order of the Garter still exists. The female equivalent of a knight is a dame. The knights of the Round Table existed until the nineteenth century.

337. Which strange structure can be found in the middle of the Place du Carrousel in Paris?

338. According to the Gospel of Luke, out of whom did Jesus drive seven devils?

339. The French kings of which family were known as the "long-haired kings"?

340. In which work by Chrétien de Troyes is the earliest known mention of the Holy Grail to be found?

341. Where in Britain, according to many legends, was Joseph of Arimathea buried?

342. The founding member of a well-known conservative religious organization wrote in a book, "Blessed be pain. Loved be pain. Sanctified be pain." Who was he?

343. The Wailing Wall in Jerusalem is said to be all that remains of which place of worship?

344. Where can a representation of a female pope be found?

345. What is an Opus Dei numerary?

346. Which Italian painter and artist, some of whose work is displayed in the Louvre, murdered a man named Ranuccio Tomassoni and fled from prosecution?

347. What is the Greek word for wisdom?

348. Fache attempts to track Langdon using GPS technology; what does GPS stand for, and how does it work?

349. Where might you visit the Chapel of Golgotha and the supposed site of Jesus's resurrection?

350. Which Spanish priest was born in 1902, died in 1975, and was made a saint in 2002?

351. Which country lies in the Pyrenees between France and Spain?

352. Which religious texts were discovered by bedouin in a cave in 1947?

353. From which organization do the London legal institutions known as the Inner Temple and the Middle Temple get their name?

354. Which book by Josemaría Escrivá lists 999 points for doing God's work?

355. In traditional Christian biblical scholarship, the "End of Days" prophecy describes a time when whose judgment will be meted out?

356. What is the purpose of the gnomon in Saint-Sulpice?

357. Which London park is home to pelicans that are descendants of a gift to Charles II?

358. What is the name of Paris's prestigious tennis stadium?

359. The original prime meridian, or Rose Line, was measured and marked out by which scientist, commonly thought of as the founder of French astronomy?

360. True or false: The Heckler & Koch USP 40 handgun used by Silas in Dan Brown's novel is a fully automatic weapon.

361. Which famous artwork took Leonardo da Vinci four years to paint but took craftsmen five times longer to restore—from 1979 to 1999?

362. Who, on Christmas Day 1066, was the first monarch to be crowned in Westminster Abbey?

363. Which capital is known as the Eternal City?

364. How is Karol Jósef Wojtyla better known?

365. Where are the Pyx Chamber, the Chapter House, and Saint Faith's Chapel located?

366. What was the name of the smallest of the twelve tribes of Israel, which in turn took its name from the youngest and favorite son of the patriarch Jacob?

367. What is London's only circular church?

368. London's National Gallery houses the alternative version of Leonardo's *Madonna of the Rocks* (held by the Louvre). What is its name?

369. By what name is Saint Matthew's Collegiate Church better known?

370. Who was Vitruvius?

371. True or false: The fleur-de-lis has been used as a symbol by Christians, the French monarchy, and the city of Florence.

372. In which country did Leonardo da Vinci die in 1517?

373. What is Big Ben?

374. What shape is Westminster Abbey's Chapter House?

375. Which master of classical mechanics used prisms to discover that white light is made up of the colors of the rainbow?

376. Sir Christopher Wren worked on the restoration of Temple Church after the Great Fire of London in 1666. His most famous building, however, is the great London church he built on the site of another that had also been destroyed in the fire. What is it?

377. What are the Nag Hammadi Gospels also known as?

378. What is the name of the archangel protecting John the Baptist in Leonardo's painting *Madonna of the Rocks*?

379. True or false: A Rose Line runs through Saint-Sulpice Church in Paris, and is marked with a brass strip.

380. What is the only "personal prelature" (to date) of the Catholic Church?

381. In 2005, what specific task did the late Pope John Paul II appoint Cardinal Tarcisio Bertone, the Archbishop of Genoa, to carry out?

382. What happened to Jacques de Molay in 1314?

383. What are the two missing figures in this sequence: 34, 55, 89, 144, –, 377, 610, –, 1547, 2584?

384. Where is the ancient Greek sculpture *Winged Victory* exhibited?

385. The abbé of the church at Rennes-le-Château allegedly discovered something in his church in 1891 that brought him untold wealth and made him famous among Grail hunters. What name does the real-life abbé share with one of the characters in *The Da Vinci Code*?

386. Where do the Swiss Guard carry out their duties?

387. Which Egyptian god is the son of Isis and Osiris?

388. Whose previously lost notebooks were published in 1974 as *The Madrid Codices*?

389. What was the name of the legendary female pope?

390. Where in the Vatican is a petition from Henry VIII of England to the Pope asking for his marriage to be annulled located?

391. In which art museum is Leonardo's painting *The Adoration of the Magi*?

392. The last alleged Grand Master of the Priory of Sion, Pierre Plantard, claimed descent from which dynasty of French kings?

393. Which symbol was used by King Clovis of France, featured on Joan of Arc's standard, and is sometimes seen on compasses?

394. True or false: Andorra is the site of a large French-run prison.

395. What were Boaz and Jachin?

396. The church of Vezelay in Burgundy claimed in the 1050s to have discovered whose remains, after her supposed escape to Gaul following Christ's death?

397. Which European city has a famous Latin Quarter?

398. What is a Manurhin MR-93?

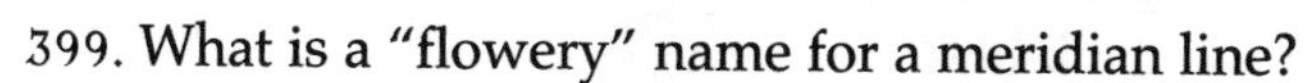

399. What is a "flowery" name for a meridian line?

400. Which organization has its Paris residence on either the Rue de Miromesnil or Rue La Bruyère?

401. What does the title of the book *Malleus maleficarum* mean?

402. On which square is the Hôtel Ritz, Paris?

403. List the first ten numbers in the Fibonacci sequence.

404. "Purge me with hyssop and I shall be clean" is a quotation from which book of the Bible?

405. The Nag Hammadi scrolls are written in which language, thought to be closest to the lost language of the ancient Egyptians?

406. Which language is described in *The Da Vinci Code* as *la lingua pura*?

407. True or false: Rosslyn is so named because it lies on a Rose Line?

408. Who was the first scientist to be knighted in Britain?

409. Which London landmark has held the coronation of almost every English (and later, British) monarch from William the Conqueror to the present day?

410. In Revelation what is "the number of the beast"?

411. What is a gnomon?

412. True or false: Jaguar manufactures "stretch" versions of its cars.

413. What was destroyed around 900 B.C.E., but is said to lie beneath the site in Jerusalem where the original Knights Templar had their headquarters?

414. True or false: There is a huge underground chamber beneath Rosslyn Chapel in Scotland.

415. Harris Tweed is woven in which group of islands off the west coast of Scotland?

416. Which tarot card depicts a woman in clerical dress and is supposed to represent hidden knowledge?

417. What has its address at 2 Avenue Gabriel, Paris, close to the Place de la Concorde?

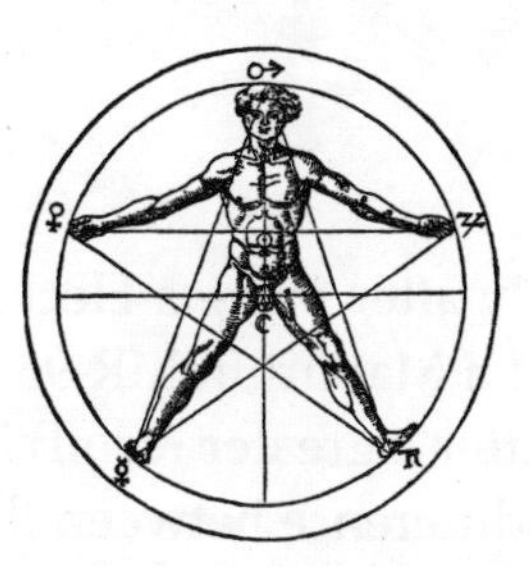

418. Which knight was employed by England's Royal Mint to track down forgers?

419. What name is given to the period between the fourteenth and sixteenth centuries that, in Europe, saw a revival of classical art and literature?

420. Which Parisian church has two towers, one of which remains unfinished?

421. Why is it incorrect to describe Newton's monument in Westminster Abbey as a tomb?

422. Immediately after firing a Heckler & Koch USP 40 and a Manurhin MR-93, what (apart from the latter's greater recoil) is the most noticeable difference between them?

423. Which English king and saint founded and was canonized in Westminster Abbey?

424. Which famous artwork can be found in the convent church of Santa Maria delle Grazie in Milan, Italy?

425. With his central tenets the worship of both a Mother Goddess and the "Horned God," Gerald Brousseau Gardner, a retired civil servant, published a book in the 1950s called *Witchcraft Today* and started a movement. What is the movement known as?

426. Formerly situated in France, what was moved to Greenwich, England, in 1888?

427. Which painting by Leonardo da Vinci is known in French as *La Joconde*?

428. What is the Ark of the Covenant?

429. What is the connection between the painting *The Penitent Magdalene* and Disney's film *The Little Mermaid*?

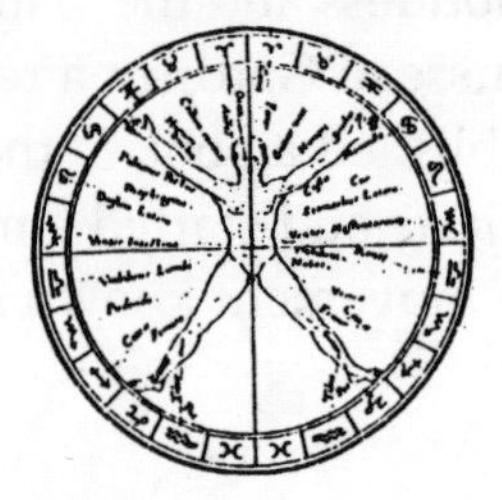

430. Which of Leonardo's works is marked at the bottom with fractions measuring the human body?

431. How many cards are there in a standard tarot deck?

432. Which ancient society of mathematicians used the pentacle as a symbol of the society?

433. Which post–World War II French president was nicknamed the Fox?

434. Which eighteenth-century composer wrote the *Masonic Funeral Music*?

435. What temple, in the ancient city of Ephesus, was one of the seven wonders of the ancient world?

436. Which famous biblical character demanded John the Baptist's head on a platter—and was obliged?

437. In ancient Egypt, what did the ankh (a cross with a loop at the top) symbolize?

438. Many religious institutions in Britain and across Europe claim possession of various parts of this saint's remains, but Abbeville Cathedral in France alleges to have her skull?

439. What is the mathematical significance of the shell of a nautilus (a species of mollusk)?

440. Which of Leonardo's works began to deteriorate while he was still alive because of the experimental medium he used to paint it?

441. Which pope survived an assassination attempt in 1981?

442. Which real French château is the fictional home of Sir Leigh Teabing in *The Da Vinci Code*?

443. True or false: The Council of Nicaea was convened to decide whether Jesus had actually existed.

444. Which church besides the Roman Church has a pope?

445. Which city is known as the City of Light?

446. Which event is announced with the Latin words *"Habemus Papam"*?

447. What is the literal meaning of the Latin phrase *sub rosa*?

448. What is the longest building in Europe?

449. What is iambic pentameter?

450. Which of the following statements is false: The ancient Greeks used five circles as a symbol for their Olympic Games. The fish has been used as a Christian symbol for centuries. The fleur-de-lis was used to represent the Holy Trinity.

451. Where is the black marble pyramid that, in *The Da Vinci Code,* supposedly marks the site of the Holy Grail?

452. True or false: A SmartCar is just over eight feet long.

453. The gnomon in Saint-Sulpice Church is a part of which commemorative structure?

454. Royal Holloway College, Sophie Neveu's alma mater, is a college of which university?

455. What is another name for Leonardo's drawing *The Proportions of the Human Figure*?

456. Which 1988 film by Martin Scorsese led to worldwide protests and a ban by the Vatican?

457. The Research Institute in Systematic Theology is run by the Department of Theology and Religious Studies of which London University college?

458. What was *La Guerre d'Algérie*?

459. In which European museum is the Richelieu Wing?

460. Which mathematical genius was honored by being made a guest at the court of the Holy Roman Emperor Frederick II in the thirteenth century?

461. Which English fourteenth-century Romance poem features a hero with a pentagram-engraved shield?

462. What is the name of the Greek counterpart of the Roman goddess Venus?

463. Where are the Salle des États and the Salle Rembrandt located?

464. What is the name given to a five-pointed star shape?

465. What is a *stylo de lumière noire*?

466. Which popular painting in the Louvre is thought, by some, to be a portrait of the artist in drag?

467. Which London tourist attraction features on the Bayeux Tapestry?

468. Which secret society, founded by Christian Rosenkreuz in the seventeenth century, had a rose and a cross as its symbols?

469. A circle surmounting an equal-armed cross is the astrological sign of which planet?

470. The names of two of the authors of *Holy Blood, Holy Grail,* Michael Baigent and Richard Leigh, are used in the name of which fictional character in *The Da Vinci Code*?

471. What is the artist Sandro Botticelli's connection with the Priory of Sion?

472. What is the meaning of the Latin verb *cruciare*?

473. Which organization enables police cooperation between different countries?

474. Which "Pope" wrote poems, satires, and epithets and translated classical literature into English?

475. Why is Jerusalem a holy place for Muslims?

476. Which feature of the Louvre complex has been described as a "remarkable anti-structure" and in *The Da Vinci Code* as an expression of the masculine?

477. Which of the following were Freemasons: Richard Wagner, Ludwig van Beethoven, and Wolfgang Amadeus Mozart?

478. Who presided over the knights of the Round Table?

479. What is the meaning of the French phrase *preuve de mérite*?

480. Where are the headquarters of the Metropolitan Police Service, responsible for policing Greater London?

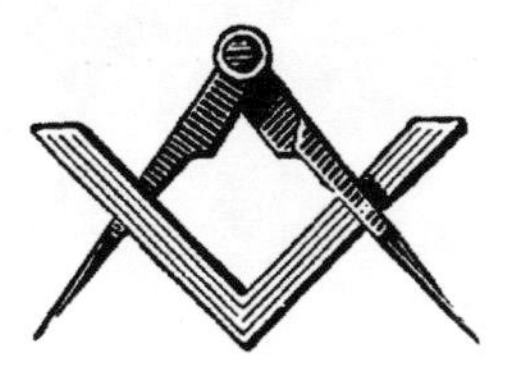

481. What is the French word for "blood"?

482. How are the Knights Templar commemorated in London's transport system?

483. Which book by Margaret Starbird is about Mary Magdalene and the Holy Grail and features in Sir Leigh Teabing's fictional study?

484. Which female saint's feast day falls on July 22?

485. True or false: Leonardo da Vinci called his painting the *Mona Lisa*.

486. What does the Greek word *gnosis* mean?

487. *The Hunchback of Notre Dame* is one of whose most famous novels?

488. In *The Da Vinci Code,* Sir Leigh Teabing finds it necessary to smuggle escargots into Britain. What are they?

489. Which religious figure is associated with a lotus blossom?

490. Who wrote the opera *Parsifal*?

491. True or false: The Romans called the study of anagrams *ars magna* ("the great art").

492. "Solomon's Seal" is a name for the Jewish symbol better known as what?

493. What does the Hopi Indian word *koyaanisqatsi* mean?

494. Which moment in Jesus's life does *The Last Supper* portray?

495. What is the sfumato style?

496. How is Joseph Ratzinger better known?

497. Where can you find Castel Sant'Angelo?

498. Which twentieth-century French president began a large-scale expansion of the Louvre?

499. Which artist painted *Death of the Virgin*, which hangs in the Louvre's Grande Galerie along with several of his other paintings?

500. How was the Temple Church badly damaged in the twentieth century?

501. In which Tuscan city is the Hotel Brunelleschi?

The Answers

1. Biggin Hill.
2. According to the *Dossiers Secrets,* they are all supposed to be past Grand Masters of the Priory of Sion.
3. *The Last Supper*.
4. True. Two rival popes were elected in 1378, one residing in Avignon and the other in Rome; a third was elected to try and end the schism.
5. Mary Magdalene.
6. The Knights Templar.
7. Opus Dei.
8. It lasted just thirty-three days, from August 26 to September 28, 1978.
9. Leonardo da Vinci.
10. Salvador Dalí.
11. Peter.
12. The fact that it was established by King George III in 1829.

13. Rome.

14. The Gnostic Gospels, or Nag Hammadi Gospels.

15. Leonardo da Vinci.

16. The Louvre's glass pyramid.

17. The Dome of the Rock.

18. Silas.

19. The order to arrest the Knights, which led to the torture and execution of most of them, was given on Friday October 13, 1307.

20. Sir Isaac Newton.

21. True.

22. The Opus Dei Awareness Network, which draws attention to and makes public the aspects of Opus Dei that it considers dangerous.

23. Job.

24. "I punish my body."

25. Castel Gandolfo.

26. Rosslyn Chapel.

27. The Pompidou Centre.
28. Saint-Sulpice.
29. Leonardo da Vinci.
30. The London Eye (or Millennium Eye, as it is called in *The Da Vinci Code*).
31. David Teniers the Younger.
32. Castel Gandolfo.
33. The Church of the Holy Sepulchre in Jerusalem.
34. "God's work."
35. *The Last Supper* (the Italian translates as "Vincian Supper").
36. Peter.
37. Mary Magdalene.
38. The first statement is false. Godefroi de Bouillon was a French duke who fought in the First Crusade.
39. A movable feast.
40. The Gnostic Gospels (the Gospel of Philip).
41. The Vatican Bank.

42. False. The founding of the Knights Templar took place nineteen years after Godefroi de Bouillon's death.

43. Judas.

44. President François Mitterrand.

45. Leonardo da Vinci.

46. Dolly, the world's first cloned animal, was born in 1997 at the Roslin Institute, in the same village as the chapel.

47. True.

48. Saint Paul's.

49. The pope's.

50. Sir Isaac Newton.

51. The Knights Hospitaller (also known as the Knights of Malta and the Knights of Saint John). The organization exists to this day.

52. Underneath the main altar of Saint Peter's Basilica in the Vatican.

53. The Knights Templar. The Priory of Sion seems to have been invented in the 1950s by Pierre Plantard. There is no evidence of its existence before 1956.

54. The *Mona Lisa*.

55. "Do not disturb."

56. *Holy Blood, Holy Grail*.

57. Phi.

58. Opus Dei.

59. *The Last Supper*.

60. Plexiglas (U.S.), also called Perspex (UK).

61. A collection of notes made by Leonardo da Vinci in his mirror-image handwriting.

62. Sir Isaac Newton.

63. Joseph of Arimathea.

64. A sixteenth-century Italian noblewoman, believed to be the subject of the *Mona Lisa*.

65. The Borgias (Rodrigo Borgia took the name Alexander VI).

66. Byzantium (the site of modern Istanbul).

67. The *Mona Lisa*.

68. The Gospel of John.

69. It is thought to be derived from the town of Magdala, by the Sea of Galilee.

70. The Bibliothèque Nationale de France (National Library of France).

71. Florence.

72. It was a frontline Royal Air Force fighter station and played an important part in the British victory over the German Luftwaffe.

73. There isn't one; the position does not exist.

74. It serves as a skylight for the underground area beneath it.

75. True.

76. A spiked belt worn around the thigh, said to be worn by full-time members of Opus Dei for part of each day.

77. In a tarot deck.

78. False. The painting was taken down so that Seracini could examine it.

79. Pierre Plantard.

80. The Atbash Cipher.

81. A prostitute, an interpretation issued by Pope Gregory I.

82. Saint-Sulpice.

83. Hieronymous Bosch.

84. Paris. The medallions mark the original prime meridian line.

85. Sir Isaac Newton's.

86. False. The chapel was founded by Sir William Saint Clair, earl of Rosslyn and Orkney, in the 1400s.

87. *Direction Centrale de la Police Judiciare*, the French internal-security police.

88. Constantine the Great.

89. François Mitterrand.

90. The Knights Templar.

91. Saint-Sulpice.

92. "Throat." In modern French *gargouille* means "gargoyle" or "waterspout."

93. She does not have any.

94. Constantine the Great (who was baptized as a Christian just a year before his death).

95. Sir Isaac Newton.

96. Leonardo da Vinci (also known as Fiumicino) and Ciampino.

97. *The Last Supper*.

98. It is a mural: A fresco is painted on fresh (*fresco*) plaster before it is dry; a mural is painted on top of dry plaster.

99. False.

100. False. It is an invention by Dan Brown.

101. Sandro Botticelli.

102. The fact that he was dead by the time the films were made.

103. Baphomet.

104. A cross embedded with thirteen gems.

105. King Arthur.

106. Ephesus.

107. Rosslyn Chapel.

108. Osiris.

109. The Sorbonne.

110. True.

111. The *Mona Lisa,* when it was stolen in 1911.

112. Venus.

113. The Dead Sea Scrolls.

114. In the Church of the Holy Sepulchre, in Jerusalem.

115. Avignon.

116. False.

117. Vatican City.

118. From Temple Mount in Jerusalem.

119. The Seine.

120. True.

121. Leonardo da Vinci.

122. Temple Church.

123. Dominique-François-Jean Arago.

124. King Dagobert II.

125. Opus Dei.

126. True.

127. The Jardin des Tuileries.

128. *Julius Caesar* (1599).

129. False. They are Jewish.

130. Mary, Queen of Scots.

131. Paul (or Saul as he was called before his baptism).

132. Westminster Abbey, London.

133. The pope.

134. The Knights Templar.

135. John Paul I.

136. Le Bourget.

137. Castel Gandolfo.

138. Taurus.

139. Royal Holloway and Bedford New College.

140. The Salle des États.

141. Phi (ϕ).

142. False. According to the Louvre, there are 673; according to the architect's office, there are 698.

143. Saint James's Park.

144. Sir Isaac Newton.

145. The London Eye, (or Millennium Eye as it is called in *The Da Vinci Code*).

146. Saint Peter.

147. The family is supposed to be descended from Jesus and Mary Magdalene.

148. True.

149. Saint-Sulpice. The initials stand for "Pierre" and "Sulpice" rather than the "Priory of Sion", however.

150. The *Mona Lisa*.

151. John the Baptist.

152. False. It is more like sixty miles to the gallon.

153. Wands, Cups, Swords, and Pentacles.

154. "Five words."

155. Napoleon Bonaparte.

156. He found that layers of overpainting obscure a completely different painting underneath and that none of the visible painting was done by Leonardo.

157. Wolfgang Amadeus Mozart.

158. Mary Magdalene. King Charles of Anjou claimed to have found her bones there in the thirteenth century.

159. Saint Mary's Hospital, near Paddington Station.

160. In Rosslyn Chapel. (There is no Mason's Pillar, however.)

161. The first council of the church. Held in what is now Turkey in the fourth century C.E. and presided over by Constantine the Great, the council made decisions on various aspects of Christianity.

162. Thirteen.

163. Florence.

164. Temple Church.

165. *Malleus Maleficarum*, or *The Hammer of Witches*.

166. Temple Mount.

167. Mithras.

168. The Carrousel du Louvre.

169. Nicolas Poussin.

170. False. Approved scholars can visit the archives. No browsing is allowed, however; they must ask specifically for what they wish to read.

171. The last Grand Master of the Knights Templar.

172. The Virgin Birth.

173. *The Last Supper*.

174. The American University of Paris.

175. False. They were held in honor of Zeus. In any case, Venus is the Roman name for the Greek goddess Aphrodite.

176. Temple Church.

177. Poseidon.

178. Pablo Picasso.

179. The first statement is false.

180. True.

181. Constantinople.

182. Coptic (not Aramaic, as Teabing states in *The Da Vinci Code*).

183. Roofing tiles (*tuiles*).

184. Because Solomon's Temple had been destroyed centuries before Rosslyn Chapel was built and no one could know what it looked like.

185. False.

186. Christ's resurrection.

187. Temple Church.

188. Georges de la Tour.

189. He claimed he stole it out of patriotism—the painting was by an Italian and should be returned to Italy. He also wrongly believed that it had been looted from Italy by Napoleon's troops and brought to France; in fact, Leonardo himself took the painting to France, where he died.

190. False. Only thirteen (at most) paintings attributed to Leonardo are extant.

191. Emperor Constantine the Great. The vision he claimed to have seen came shortly before his victory at the Battle of Milvian Bridge, and as a direct result of this Constantine later converted to Christianity.

192. Saint John.

193. True. Vatican City is so small that there is no room for the embassy.

194. Pierre Plantard.

195. In a tarot deck. There are twenty-two cards in the Major Arcana and fifty-six in the Minor Arcana.

196. A large forested park in Paris.

197. The Gnostic Gospels.

198. John Paul II.

199. A keystone.

200. Because a non-British subject who has been knighted is not permitted to use the title, only the initials after his name—in this case, Rudy Giuliani, KBE (Knight of the British Empire).

201. Nine.

202. An aircraft (Bishop Aringarosa flies in one from Rome in *The Da Vinci Code*). A twin-engine propeller-driven machine introduced in the 1970s, it is popular as an executive transport.

203. True. Pierre Plantard, the self-appointed Grand Master of the Priory of Sion, used the symbol because it had been one of the badges of the French monarchy.

204. In the center of the Place de la Concorde, Paris's largest square. It is known as the Obelisk of Luxor or (as it is in *The Da Vinci Code*) the Obelisk of Ramses.

205. Egypt.

206. Unlike the vast majority of national flags, it is a square rather than a rectangle.

207. Ieoh Ming Pei.

208. Sir Christopher Wren.

209. True. Pierre Plantard registered the organization in the 1950s.

210. Bill Gates.

211. The Gregorian calendar, after it was promulgated by Pope Gregory XIII.

212. The American University of Paris.

213. Because "da Vinci" means "of Vinci." It is not a surname; Vinci is a small town in Tuscany, Italy, and the birthplace of Leonardo.

214. Jesus's.

215. Poets' Corner, in Westminster Abbey.

216. Documents relating to the Priory of Sion, among them a history of the society and a list of its Grand Masters.

217. Leonardo da Vinci.

218. Hebrew.

219. Elizabeth I.

220. Wicca.

221. Underneath Rosslyn Chapel.

222. The National Gallery, in London.

223. False: She is mentioned only twelve times.

224. The Arians.

225. Leonardo did not design a cryptex. The cryptex is an invention of Dan Brown's in *The Da Vinci Code*.

226. "I do the work of God" (uttered by Silas in *The Da Vinci Code*).

227. A ninth-century Arab scientist, philosopher, and expert on codes and ciphers.

228. As the story goes, after Newton was hit on the head by an apple, he began to think about the force that made it fall—gravity. Almost certainly apocryphal the story was related to the French writer and historian Voltaire by Newton's niece after the scientist's death.

229. The Musée d'Orsay.

230. *Angels and Demons*.

231. Vatican City.

232. Opus Dei.

233. True. The year before he became pope in 1378, he had ordered the execution of 4,000 people in the northern Italian town of Cesena.

234. The Gare du Nord. In the first edition of *The Da Vinci Code* Sophie and Robert buy their tickets from Gare Saint-Lazare, but in subsequent editions the error has been corrected. The Gare Saint-Lazare serves northwestern France, whereas Lille is to the northeast of Paris.

235. Kensington Gardens.

236. Opus Dei.

237. False.

238. *Eyes Wide Shut*.

239. Florence.

240. The Swiss Guard.

241. The Arc de Triomphe.

242. Leonardo da Vinci.

243. Jean Cocteau.

244. Claude Monet.

245. Silas.

246. In 1969 (about 1,400 years after Pope Gregory I made the statement).

247. True.

248. "Red herring" (although a literal translation is "pink herring").

249. Chartres Cathedral.

250. Leonardo Fibonacci.

251. The Vatican Secret Archives.

252. The Louvre.

253. The Chapter House.

254. The Second Vatican Council, or Vatican II.

255. Peter.

256. True.

257. False. Pope did write an epitaph for Newton, however: "Nature and Nature's laws lay hid in night / God said, 'let Newton be!' and all was light."

258. Westminster Abbey.

259. The Eiffel Tower.

260. The Gospel of Philip (one of the Gnostic Gospels).

261. Rosslyn Chapel.

262. Ephesus (Mary is believed by some to have traveled there after the Crucifixion).

263. The *Codex Leicester* (a collection of notes by Leonardo da Vinci).

264. The last statement is false.

265. *The Way* (its original title was *Spiritual Considerations*).

266. Isis.

267. Avignon, France.

268. Saint Paul's Cathedral.

269. A series of brass medallions marking the original prime meridian line in Paris. The line is named after the astronomer who established its position.

270. The Gospel of Mark.

271. The Golden Ratio (or Golden Number or Divine Proportion).

272. True.

273. Rome.

274. *The Last Temptation of Christ*.

275. The Louvre.

276. Philipe IV of France, also known as Philip the Fair.

277. True.

278. The Greek god of love.

279. "Sacred/divine marriage".

280. Vatican City.

281. The Nicene Creed.

282. True.

283. The Merovingians.

284. The twelfth century C.E.

285. Leonardo da Vinci.

286. True.

287. The five wounds of Christ.

288. The Vatican.

289. False. Estimates vary greatly, but it is thought that, at the most, perhaps 100,000 people were executed as witches, not all of them women, and most were not burned at the stake.

290. It is an act of voluntary self-punishment in atonement for perceived wrongdoings.

291. Istanbul.

292. Keystone.

293. False. Fruit, vegetables, and medicinal herbs were grown there.

294. The Gospel of John.

295. The Priory of Sion (and afterwards the Knights Templar).

296. "Q" (referred to in *The Da Vinci Code* as "the legendary Q Document").

297. The letters of Paul in the New Testament.

298. Saint James's Park.

299. The building is Temple Church, and it is situated adjacent to two of the London Inns of Court—the Middle Temple and the Inner Temple—both of which are historic "training grounds" for British barristers and lawyers.

300. The building in the center of the picture is an impression of the Temple of Solomon. Legend has it that on arriving in Jerusalem, the Knights Templar established their camp on the site that the temple had once occupied and promptly began to excavate below the surface. Some scholars theorize that the treasures allegedly discovered during these excavations—priceless documents and scrolls of ancient knowledge and perhaps even the Ark of the Covenant itself—were the source of the Templars' wealth.

301. Tempera.

302. Bois de Boulogne.

303. It is a SmartCar, built by Mercedes-Benz.

304. The Chapter House.

305. Rosslyn Chapel.

306. The *Codex Leicester* (after the Earl of Leicester who bought it in the eighteenth century).

307. The Arc de Triomphe.

308. Baphomet.

309. The Essenes, who lived in Palestine from the second century B.C.E. to the first century C.E.

310. A thin sheet of poplar wood.

311. In Westminster Abbey, it is Sir Isaac Newton's monument.

312. In Saint-Sulpice.

313. Because he is a Knight Templar; the order's formal designation was The Poor Knights of Christ and of the Temple of Solomon.

314. The Tarot.

315. King Solomon.

316. Seven.

317. Version B is the earlier; sometimes known as *Virgin of the Rocks,* it is displayed in the Louvre.

318. *The Last Supper.*

319. The Priory of Sion, according to the *Dossiers Secrets.*

320. Saint Stephen (the holiday is Boxing Day).

321. Blackfriars Bridge.

322. Georgia O'Keeffe.

323. Vatican City (although Italian is often used).

324. *Draconian.*

325. Approximately 65,000.

326. Both points are true.

327. Vatican City.

328. Leonardo da Vinci's.

329. Twenty-seven.

330 Château Villette.

331. Aramaic.

332. The twentieth century; there is only evidence of the society's existence from 1956.

333. The Chapter House, in Westminster Abbey.

334. Cardinal Ratzinger, who took the name Pope Benedict XVI.

335. Baphomet was supposed to be a pagan idol.

336. The last statement is false.

337. The Pyramide Inversée (upside-down pyramid).

338. Mary Magdalene.

339. The Merovingians (no one knows the significance of the long hair).

340. *Perceval.*

341. Glastonbury.

342. Josemaría Escrivá. The book is *The Way*.

343. Solomon's Temple.

344. In a tarot deck (the card is also referred to as the High Priestess).

345. A full-time member of the organization who (usually) lives in an Opus Dei residence and practices celibacy.

346. Michelangelo Merisi da Caravaggio, usually known simply as Caravaggio.

347. *Sofia*.

348. GPS stands for Global Positioning System, and it works by determining the user's location utilizing information gathered from a numbeffr of satellites orbiting the Earth.

349. The Church of the Holy Sepulchre in Jerusalem.

350. Josemaría Escrivá.

351. Andorra.

352. The Dead Sea Scrolls.

353. The Knights Templar.

354. *The Way*.

355. God's.

356. To determine the exact date of the spring and autumn equinoxes, so as to correctly calculate the date of Easter.

357. Saint James's Park.

358. Roland-Garros.

359. Jean Picard (1620–1682).

360. False. It is a self-loading, or semiautomatic, pistol (semiautomatics are often incorrectly referred to as automatics).

361. *The Last Supper*.

362. William the Conqueror.

363. Rome.

364. Pope John Paul II.

365. In Westminster Abbey.

366. Benjamin (in the novel, Mary Magdalene is said to be of the tribe of Benjamin).

367. Temple Church.

368. *Virgin of the Rocks*.

369. Rosslyn Chapel.

370. A Roman architect who explained his ideas on ideal human and architectural proportions in his work *De architectura*.

371. True.

372. France.

373. The hour bell of the Great Clock of Westminster, situated in the Palace of Westminster in London.

374 Octagonal.

375. Sir Isaac Newton.

376. Saint Paul's Cathedral.

377. The Gnostic Gospels.

378. Uriel.

379. False. The brass line on the floor of the church is part of the gnomon, a device for measuring the angle of the sun. The Rose Line runs close to the church but not through it.

380. Opus Dei.

381. He was appointed by the Vatican to refute the "shameful and unfounded errors" about the Catholic church contained within *The Da Vinci Code.*

382. He was burned at the stake.

383. 233, 987. In the Fibonacci sequence, each number is the sum of the two preceding numbers: 89 + 144 = 233; 377 + 610 = 987.

384. The Louvre.

385. Saunière.

386. In Vatican City.

387. Horus.

388. Leonardo da Vinci's.

389. Pope Joan.

390. The Vatican Secret Archives.

391. The Uffizi Gallery, in Florence.

392. The Merovingians.

393. The fleur-de-lis.

394. False. Andorra is an independent country between France and Spain.

395. Two pillars that stood at the gates of Solomon's Temple. (In *The Da Vinci Code,* two of the pillars in Rosslyn Chapel are interpreted as being copies of Boaz and Jachin.)

396. Mary Magdalene's.

397. Paris.

398. A revolver, carried by Bezu Fache and the standard-issue weapon of the French police.

399. Rose Line.

400. Opus Dei. (In *The Da Vinci Code*, the residence is on Rue La Bruyère.)

401. *The Hammer of Witches* (or *The Witches' Hammer*).

402. The Place Vendôme.

403. 0, 1, 1, 2, 3, 5, 8, 13, 21, 34.

404. Psalms. (In *The Da Vinci Code*, Silas quotes the words as he cleans his own blood, the result of self-flagellation.)

405. Coptic.

406. English.

407. False. The name Rosslyn derives from *ross* meaning "hill" and *lynn* meaning "water" (the chapel is built on a hill above a river).

408. Sir Isaac Newton.

409. Westminster Abbey. (There are two exceptions—Edward V and Edward VIII.)

410. 666.

411. An instrument dating from ancient times and used to calculate the exact time of year from the angle of the sun; it is also the projecting piece on a sundial that shows the time by the position of the shadow it casts.

412. False. Such versions are built to order for individual clients by specialist companies.

413. The Temple of Solomon.

414. False. (Though the crypt of the Saint Clair [Sinclair] family lies underneath the north aisle.)

415. The Outer Hebrides.

416. The Female Pope, or High Priestess.

417. The U.S. Embassy.

418. Sir Isaac Newton.

419. Renaissance.

420. Saint-Sulpice.

421. Because Newton's body is not buried inside it (although he is buried nearby, in front of the choir screen).

422. The USP 40—a semiautomatic, or self-loading, pistol—automatically ejects the spent cartridge case and loads a fresh round; the MR-93, a revolver, does not.

423. Edward the Confessor.

424. Leonardo da Vinci's *The Last Supper*.

425. Wicca.

426. The prime meridian.

427. The *Mona Lisa*.

428. A chest containing the stone tablets of the Ten Commandments.

429. A replica of the painting is hanging in the mermaid Ariel's home in the film.

430. *Vitruvian Man*.

431. Traditionally there are seventy-eight (not twenty-two as mentioned in *The Da Vinci Code*).

432. The Pythagoreans.

433. President François Mitterrand.

434. Wolfgang Amadeus Mozart.

435. The Temple of Artemis (Diana, to the Romans).

436. Salome.

437. Life.

438. Mary Magdalene's.

439. The pattern of the spirals in its shell conforms to the Golden Ratio.

440. *The Last Supper*.

441. Pope John Paul II.

442. Château Villette.

443. False. The council was convened to take a vote on the status of Jesus's divinity.

444. The Coptic Church.

445. Paris.

446. The election of a new pope (the words mean "We have a Pope!").

447. "Under the rose." Dialogue spoken *sub rosa* is intended to be secret.

448. The Louvre.

449. A poetic meter with five iambs (pairs of stressed and unstressed syllables) in each line.

450. The first statement is false. The five-circles symbol was first used in the twentieth century.

451. Underneath the Place du Carrousel and the Pyramide Inversée in the Louvre.

452. True.

453. An obelisk.

454. The University of London.

455. *Vitruvian Man*.

456. *The Last Temptation of Christ*.

457. King's College.

458. The Algerian War of Independence, waged against France from 1954 to 1962, of which Saunière is a veteran.

459. The Louvre.

460. Leonardo Fibonacci.

461. *Sir Gawain and the Green Knight*.

462. Aphrodite.

463. In the Louvre.

464. Pentagram.

465. A black-light pen; marks made with a black-light pen are invisible in normal light but show up when exposed to an ultraviolet light source.

466. Leonardo da Vinci's *Mona Lisa*.

467. Westminster Abbey.

468. The Rosicrucians.

469. Venus.

470. Sir Leigh Teabing.

471. He is supposed to have been one of its Grand Masters.

472. "To torture."

473. Interpol.

474. Alexander Pope (1688–1744).

475. It was the place from which Muhammad ascended to heaven.

476. The Pyramide Inversée (by the judges of the 1995 Benedictus Awards).

477. They all were.

478. King Arthur.

479. "Proof of merit."

480. New Scotland Yard (also known simply as Scotland Yard).

481. *Sang*.

482. With the Temple underground station.

483. *The Woman with the Alabaster Jar*.

484. Saint Mary Magdalene's.

485. False. *Mona Lisa* is the English name for the work. During Leonardo's lifetime the painting did not have a title.

486. "Knowledge of the spiritual."

487. Victor Hugo's.

488. Edible snails.

489. Buddha.

490. Richard Wagner.

491. False. *Ars magna* is an anagram of the word *anagrams*.

492. Star of David.

493. "Life out of balance."

494. It portrays the moment shortly after Jesus has declared that one of his disciples will betray him before sunrise, and the resulting shock and disbelief felt by his followers.

495. A painting technique that creates a form by using a blurred image rather than hard lines. One of the best examples of the use of sfumato is found in the *Mona Lisa*.

496. As Pope Benedict XVI.

497. Rome.

498. President François Mitterrand.

499. Caravaggio.

500. In World War II, it was bombed in 1941 during the blitz.

501. Florence (Robert Langdon tells Sophie of his forthcoming trip there at the end of *The Da Vinci Code*).

Picture credits:

483: Ray Tang / Rex Features

484: Getty Images

486, 487, 495, 496: Roger-Viollet / TopFoto

488: TopFoto / Woodmansterne

489, 498: Charles Walker / TopFoto

490: Codex Leicester f. 1r: notes on the Earth and Moon, their sizes and relationships to the Sun, Vinci, Leonardo da (1452-1519) / Christies Images; / Bridgeman Art Library

491: Sipa Press / Rex Features

492: TopFoto / Fortean

493: Israelimages / Rex Features

497: Mary Evans Picture Library

499: The Art Archive / Louvre Museum, Paris / Dagli Orti

500: Dave Penman / Rex Features